over 20 true stories
of battle
and adventure

real knights

illustrations by John James

text by Christopher Gravett

ENCHANTED LION BOOKS
New York

First American Edition published in 2005 by

Enchanted Lion Books, 115 West 18th Street, New York, NY 10011

Conceived and produced by **Breslich & Foss Ltd**., London

Designed by **Balley Design Associates**

Printed and bound in China

A CIP record is available from the Library of Congress

ISBN 1 - 59270 - 034 - 9

Contents

Introduction

The knight was an important person in the Middle Ages (a period from about 500CE to 1500). While the rules governing knighthood varied between countries, it was most common for only sons of knights to be accepted into the knighthood. This changed in the later Middle Ages as nobility became less rigidly defined and money became more powerful than land.

Chivalry

GALEAS OF MANTUA

Early knights were rough fighting men who could afford horses and held land by virtue of military prowess. They began to emerge in the ninth century as the feudal system took shape and spread. Knights began to change in the twelfth century with courtly love, the cult of the Virgin Mary, the romances of King Arthur, and the birth of the idea of chivalry. Knights had to respect ladies, and protect the poor and the weak. The Italian Galeas of Mantua was supposed to be the perfect knight, but many knights still married ladies for their land rather than for love!

EARL OF WARWICK

The misuse of power

Richard Neville, the Earl of Warwick, was a powerful fifteenth-century knight and a skilled politician who was known as the "King-maker" because he had helped the future Edward IV to the English throne. However, he also ruthlessly executed captured enemy knights, which was not a chivalrous thing to do!

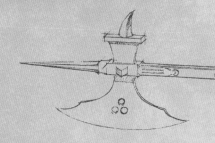

A dying breed

Knights, on account of their status as landowners, had to take part in government. Although many preferred running their estates to going to war, taking part in national government was time-consuming. This, coupled with the expense of being knighted and buying horses and equipment, led many men to avoid knighthood. In fifteenth-century England, there were only about one hundred knights left.

Early Knights

As part of the feudal system, a boy would enter a lord's household at about seven years old as a page. Next he would become a squire, and eventually a knight. As a knight, he would be expected to assist his lord for an agreed number of days per year. In return for this service, the knight could live in the lord's hall, or be given a plot of land to farm. Only the eldest son in a family could inherit the father's fortune, so a younger son's best chance of making his way in the world was to marry the daughter of a wealthy lord. From the twelfth century, many young knights took part in tournaments in a bid to win renown for their skills and so find a place in a lord's household.

A Spanish hero

A man appeared in the eleventh century who would become a national hero in Spain. His name was Rodrigo Diáz de Bivar, but he is better known today as "El Cid," from the Arabic word for "lord," or as "El Campeador," Spanish for "champion." He commanded troops for King Sancho II of Castile, but the king was assassinated during a siege in 1072 and his brother, the King of León, banished Rodrigo, who went to fight for the Muslim ruler of Zaragoza instead. Later, he again changed sides and captured Valencia from the Muslims and ruled it himself. According to legend, El Cid was killed by an arrow while defending Valencia from the Muslims in 1099. So that neither his followers nor the enemy would realize he was dead, El Cid's body was strapped onto his horse for a final charge at the enemy.

"El Cid"

7

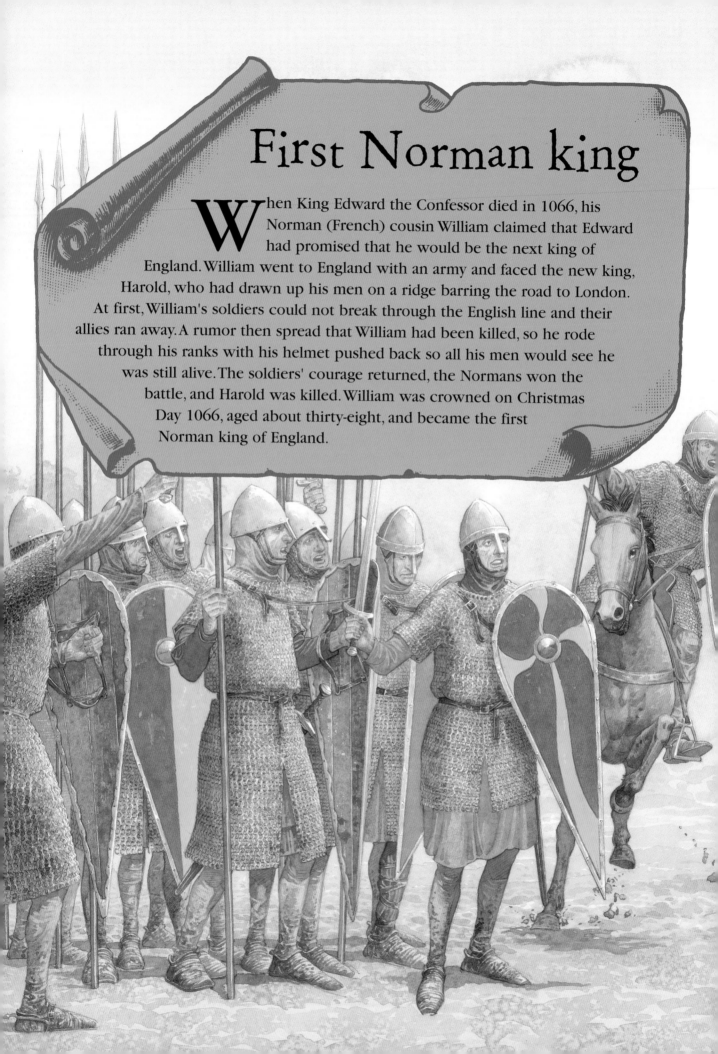

First Norman king

When King Edward the Confessor died in 1066, his Norman (French) cousin William claimed that Edward had promised that he would be the next king of England. William went to England with an army and faced the new king, Harold, who had drawn up his men on a ridge barring the road to London. At first, William's soldiers could not break through the English line and their allies ran away. A rumor then spread that William had been killed, so he rode through his ranks with his helmet pushed back so all his men would see he was still alive. The soldiers' courage returned, the Normans won the battle, and Harold was killed. William was crowned on Christmas Day 1066, aged about thirty-eight, and became the first Norman king of England.

WILLIAM THE CONQUEROR

A generous knight

Arnold was a handsome young squire who was trained in good manners and knighthood at the court of Count Philip of Flanders. After being "knighted" in 1181, Arnold gave money to a crowd of minstrels, jesters, and servants who were at the ceremony, leaving hardly anything for himself. The new knight then set off in search of adventure. He tried to marry the rich Countess of Boulogne, but was clapped in prison when he challenged the man who had won her hand. He paid a ransom to get out of prison then went home and fought alongside his father. Eventually he married a beautiful lady named Beatrice. At his court, he kept storytellers and old knights who could tell exciting stories about King Arthur, the Emperor Charlemagne, and adventures in the Holy Land.

ARNOLD OF ARDRES

His head on the block!

William Marshal was the landless younger son of an English baron who entered tournaments to make his fortune. It was the rule in tournaments that the knight who lost the contest had to hand over his horse and armor to the victor. Sometimes the winning knight also made the loser pay a ransom to be set free. William was so skilled that he gradually became very wealthy, although he had a few accidents—tournaments were rough and dangerous events. After winning one contest, William's helmet was so bashed and dented that he couldn't take it off! He had to place his head on an anvil so that the blacksmith could beat his helmet back into shape.

William was such a success that King Henry II made him tutor-in-arms to his young son, Prince Henry. William later served King Richard the "Lionheart" and King John, and looked after the kingdom for John's young son, Henry III, after the king died in 1216.

WILLIAM MARSHAL

Armor & Weapons

The well-armed knight in the eleventh century was protected by a coat of "mail," sometimes with a hood attached. Mail sleeves ending in mittens to protect the knight's hands, and mail stockings to protect his legs became popular in the twelfth century. Over the top of his mail suit and a padded coat, the knight might wear a cloth tunic or "surcoat."

Suits of armor

By 1300, armorers (the people who made armor) added plates of steel, whalebone, or hardened leather to armor. In the fifteenth century, steel plates were attached to an "arming doublet." Starting at the feet and working upward, two assistants could arm a knight in about five minutes. An armor for battle weighed about 55 pounds. As this weight was spread over the body, a fit knight could run, lie down, or mount a horse without help.

THIS FIFTEENTH-CENTURY KNIGHT IS BEING ARMED BY HIS SQUIRE. HIS ARMING DOUBLET HAS PIECES OF MAIL TO FILL GAPS BETWEEN THE SOLID PLATE ARMOR.

Weapons of war

The knight's sword was his most important weapon, although he might use a type of spear called a lance when fighting on horseback. As plate armor developed, so did steel-headed maces and war-hammers to break into it. Since many knights had to fight on foot and the slippery surface of plate armor made a shield unnecessary, the knight could use both hands to hold a long weapon, such as a pollaxe or a halberd.

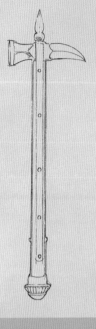

WAR-HAMMERS HAD A "BEAK" FOR PIERCING PLATE ARMOR.

MACES WERE USED TO BREAK INTO PLATE ARMOR.

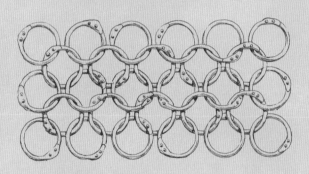

"MAIL" WAS A MESH OF SMALL, INTERLINKED IRON RINGS THAT HELPED PROTECT KNIGHTS FROM BEING CUT BY SWORDS.

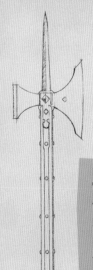

THE WOODEN SHAFT OF THIS HALBERD IS PROTECTED BY STRIPS OF STEEL. IT ALSO HAS A REAR SPIKE.

THIS FIFTEENTH-CENTURY POLLAXE HAS A HAMMER AT THE BACK.

The Crusaders

In the Middle Ages, most of the people in western Europe were Christians and belonged to the Catholic faith, whose leader was the pope. In 1095, Pope Urban II asked Christians to a join a "crusade" to recover the holy city of Jerusalem, where Jesus was buried, but which was now held by Muslims. Jerusalem was a very important place for Muslims, too, as the founder of their religion, Mohammad, had died there. Knights from all over Europe became crusaders and traveled to the Middle East to fight the Muslim soldiers, who were known as Saracens in the Holy Land and Moors in Spain. By 1099, Jerusalem had been captured by the Christians, but keeping the new land was difficult and dangerous, and many crusaders simply went home again. A new leader, whose name was Saladin (1137?-93), united all the Muslims and retook Jerusalem. There were many more crusades (including a Children's Crusade) over the next two hundred years, but the Christians never recaptured Jerusalem.

Bohemund the giant

This knight's real name was Mark, but he was such a huge baby that he was nicknamed "Bohemund" after a legendary giant. His father was one of the most ruthless Norman adventurers to conquer parts of southern Italy in the 1050s. Bohemund had blond hair and a ruddy complexion unlike his Italian neighbors who had dark hair and olive skin. Bohemund went on to become one of the leaders of the First Crusade in 1096 and besieged the great city of Antioch in Anatolia. The city was protected by Muslim soldiers in many towers around its walls, so the siege lasted for many months. Eventually the city was defeated, and Bohemund made himself the Prince of Antioch in 1100.

"Bohemund"

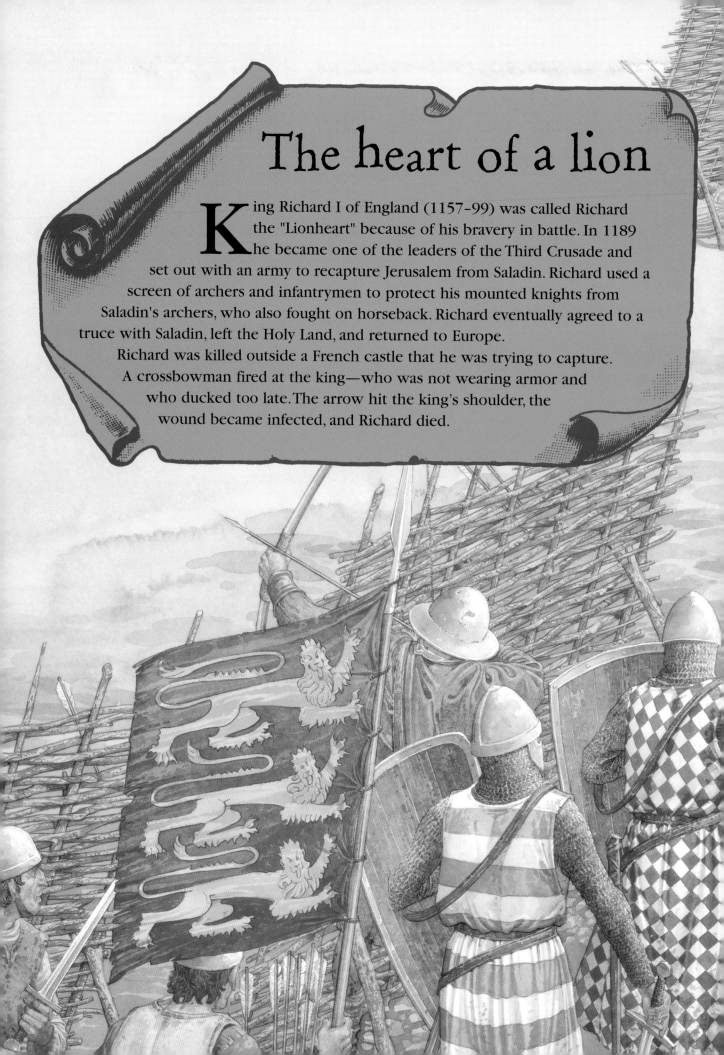

The heart of a lion

King Richard I of England (1157-99) was called Richard the "Lionheart" because of his bravery in battle. In 1189 he became one of the leaders of the Third Crusade and set out with an army to recapture Jerusalem from Saladin. Richard used a screen of archers and infantrymen to protect his mounted knights from Saladin's archers, who also fought on horseback. Richard eventually agreed to a truce with Saladin, left the Holy Land, and returned to Europe.

Richard was killed outside a French castle that he was trying to capture. A crossbowman fired at the king—who was not wearing armor and who ducked too late. The arrow hit the king's shoulder, the wound became infected, and Richard died.

RICHARD I

SIR JAMES DOUGLAS

Heart of a king

The Scottish king, Robert the Bruce, had vowed to go on crusade but had never been. When Robert died in 1329 at the age of 55, his friend, Sir James Douglas, was given a silver casket containing the king's heart, and asked to take it to the Holy Land. Sir James was called "The Good," and he accepted the challenge because it would help carry out the dead king's crusading promise.

On his journey through Spain, Sir James stopped to help the King of Castile fight against the Muslims. Sir James was hurt in the battle. Knowing that he would never reach his destination, Sir James flung the casket into the enemy ranks, shouting: "Go first as thou were wont to go!" So Robert the Bruce led his men as he had wanted to do. Still today, the Douglas family has a red heart on its coat-of-arms.

The Grand Master

The Teutonic Knights were German warrior monks who wore long white robes with a black cross on the front. When the Order was founded around 1190, the knights looked after crusaders who fell ill on their journey to the Holy Land. In 1210, Hermann von Salza became Grand Master of the Teutonic Knights and, with him as its leader, the Order soon became very wealthy and powerful. They began a religious crusade in eastern Europe, taking land from the Slavic people and trying to convert them to Christianity. Hermann von Salza built strong fortresses across the area that withstood attacks by the knights' non-Christian enemies and the Order gradually gained more and more land across what is now northern Germany and Poland.

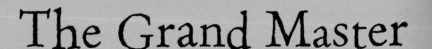

HERMANN VON SALZA

Warfare

Early knights fought on horseback, galloping close together with long spears called lances. Once through the enemy line, the knights threw down their lances and fought with double-edged swords. Sometimes, knights were ordered to dismount to help ordinary footsoldiers. This became very common in England from the fourteenth century, when small groups of knights, squires, and well-armed men stood alongside large groups of longbowmen.

Fighting methods

Mounted knights with their lances lowered could easily steamroll their way through an unprepared enemy, but footsoldiers across Europe came up with ways to stop them. In 1302, Flemish peasants charged the French cavalry before it charged them, and brought them down with clubs. English archers could shoot about twelve arrows per minute and these could bring down warhorses and pierce weak spots in men's armor. In fifteenth-century Bohemia (part of the present-day Czech republic) cannon were mounted on a barrier of wagons to beat off German knights. Men with handguns could shelter behind the wagons.

A LONGBOWMAN DRAWS HIS WEAPON. HIS ARROWS ARE STUCK IN THE GROUND SO THAT HE CAN RELOAD HIS BOW QUICKLY.

Guns and pikes

Large blocks of pikemen supported by men with guns dominated battlefields from the fifteenth to the seventeenth century, and mobile wheeled cannon were used more and more. Bullets could penetrate a steel breastplate, so the steel had to be thickened or knights had to wear two pieces of steel. In battle, armored knights with lances slowly disappeared and were replaced by lightly armored horsemen with guns and swords.

THIS FIFTEENTH-CENTURY BOHEMIAN SOLDIER LEANS ON HIS HANDGUN.

FIFTEENTH-CENTURY GERMAN AND SWISS PIKEMEN USED PIKES THAT WERE 16 FEET LONG!

Chivalry

The word "chivalry" comes from the French *cheval*, meaning "horse," and chivalry used to refer to skill with horses. Knights were ruthless fighting men, but they were also noblemen (such as kings and dukes) who could afford to fight on horseback— ordinary men had to fight on foot. In the twelfth century, the Virgin Mary became an important figure and the Church itself began to view women as pious rather than sinful temptresses. Following from this, knights were expected to be courteous towards ladies. Poems about this behavior or "courtly love," became fashionable in southern France, and gradually spread north through Europe. Minstrels called "troubadours" traveled from court to court singing love poetry in which the gallant lover hardly ever won the hand of his lady. Good manners and the importance of protecting the poor and the weak became part of the knight's chivalric code of conduct.

"Braveheart"

William Wallace was a freedom fighter to the Scots, but an outlaw in the eyes of the English, who wanted to continue their rule over Scotland. William Wallace inspired the Scots to revolt, and then raised an army that assembled near Stirling Bridge (near the border with England) in 1297. Wallace led his men in a charge that cut down enemy troops led by King Edward I of England as they crossed the narrow bridge before their comrades could join them. Some say that it was Wallace who came up with the idea of using solid groups of men with long spears to hold off the men on horseback. He was knighted after his victory at Stirling Bridge, but was defeated by King Edward in the battle of Falkirk the following year. Eventually, Wallace was betrayed to the English by jealous Scottish rivals and taken to London. After a swift trial, he suffered the agonizing traitor's death of being hanged, drawn, and quartered. The film, *Braveheart*, was loosely based on William Wallace's life.

WILLIAM WALLACE

A romantic fighter

Ulrich von Lichtenstein was a *Minnesinger*—a German knight and storyteller who traveled around telling tales of courtly love. He also wrote about his own adventures in tournaments. In 1226, he set out on a "Venus journey" to prove his love to a lady. A month later, he had broken 307 lances and given 271 rings to knights who broke a lance on him. (Knights earned points by breaking lances.) His helmet was decorated with a figure of Venus (the goddess of love) and he may even have dressed as her during his journey! Later, he devised a series of contests called the "Arthur Journey," in which each knight dressed as a character from the legendary court of King Arthur.

ULRICH VON LICHTENSTEIN.

"The Black Knight"

Zawisza Czarny's black hair and dark skin earned him the nickname, "The Black Knight." Zawisza's courage and virtue made him a folk hero in Poland, his native country, where people still talk about him. In 1410, Zawisza took part in the battle of Tannenberg against the Teutonic Knights, who wanted to win more land. At this battle, these greedy knights were beaten once and for all.

ZAWISZA CZARNY

CHEVALIER BAYARD

"Without fear and without blame"

The Chevalier Bayard wanted to be a great knight from boyhood and went down in history as the knight "Without fear and without blame." When he challenged a fierce knight, Claude de Vauldres, at a tournament, a herald at the event recorded that Bayard's beard was "not yet of three years' growth," meaning that he was still a boy. Between 1495 and 1524, Bayard fought in the wars between Italian states, but still managed to take part in tournaments. He was generous even when he had barely any money, and chivalrous: he refused to take part in a plan to poison the pope! His courage was proved when he chased an enemy band into the streets of Milan on his own and was captured. The Duke of Milan, Ludovico Sforza, was so impressed with his bravery that he let him go without a ransom. Later, he helped save France from an invading army with just a thousand men and was honored by King Francis I who invited Bayard to dub him a knight.

Castles

The first castles were built around the tenth century and were used by kings and lords to protect themselves and their families from enemies. These castles were simple enclosures protected by wooden fences and surrounded by a ditch. From the eleventh century, lords built "motte and bailey" castles. The "motte" was a mound of earth with a wooden tower on top, and the "bailey" was the enclosed courtyard.

From wood to stone

Wooden castles burnt down very easily, so in the twelfth century wealthy lords increasingly used stone to replace the wooden fences. Impressive stone towers or "keeps" also became more common. Archers could shoot at approaching enemies from smaller towers that jutted out from along the walls. "Concentric" castles developed in the thirteenth century. These had two rings of walls, which made it harder for enemies to get in—the archers on the inner walls could shoot over the heads of their companions on the lower, outer walls. In mountainous areas, castles were built on top of crags, while in flat country, moats were filled with water to stop enemies from digging mines.

A TIMBER MOTTE AND BAILEY CASTLE.

Castle entrances were heavily defended. By the thirteenth century, twin towers, metal grilles called portcullises, and drawbridges were all used to stop invaders from crossing the ditch. During sieges, enemies dug tunnels to undermine the walls, and brought ladders or wheeled towers up to the battlements. Catapults were used to pound walls or fling missiles over them.

A "TREBUCHET" WAS A HUGE CATAPULT WITH A WEIGHTED BOX. THE OTHER END SWUNG UP AND RELEASED THE MISSILE HELD IN THE SLING.

THE DOUBLE WALLS AND WIDE MOAT OF THIS CONCENTRIC CASTLE WOULD MAKE IT HARD TO INVADE.

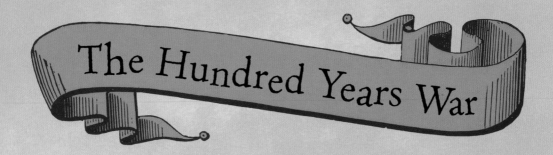

The Hundred Years War

The Hundred Years War was the name given to a conflict that broke out between England and France in 1337 and rumbled on and off until 1453—some 116 years! It was in fact a series of conflicts with quiet times in between. One of the causes of the war was the claim by Edward III of England to be king of France as well. At the time, France was shared between the two countries, and English soldiers controlled castles in northern France and Aquitaine. Over the years, the English side was victorious in major battles at Crécy, Poitiers, and Agincourt, and it looked like they would win the war. Then, a young woman called Joan of Arc came along. Joan had heard voices urging her to save France from the English. She convinced the French leader to place her at the head of the army, and her soldiers forced the English to retreat from the town of Orléans in 1439. Gradually, the English were pushed out of France until in 1453 only the town of Calais remained theirs.

The blind king

King John of Bohemia became blind with age, but when King Philip VI of France asked him to help oppose the English army, John gathered his men and joined Philip. At the battle of Crécy in 1346, the huge French army came upon a smaller English force. The English and Welsh longbowmen shot at the enemy crossbowmen, as waves of mounted French knights tried without success to break the English ranks.

King John asked his loyal knights to lead him forward so he could strike one blow with his sword. The knights tied the horses' bridles together and galloped forward. After the English victory, their bodies were found with the bridles still tied together. The victorious king, Edward III, and his son, the Black Prince, were so impressed by the bravery of King John that they attended his funeral.

KING JOHN OF BOHEMIA

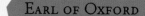

The battle of Crécy

Edward, the Black Prince, was the eldest son of King Edward III of England. He was a sixteen-year-old squire when he took part in the battle of Crécy in 1346 with the Earls of Warwick and Oxford by his side. There was a storm just before the battle that wetted the cords of the enemy's crossbows, making the weapons less effective. Then, the sun came out behind the English troops and shone in the eyes of the French, giving Edward's men another advantage. Nonetheless, the French soldiers attacked fiercely and a message was sent to King Edward saying that his son was hard-pressed. The king replied, "Let the boy win his spurs," in other words, let him earn the gold spurs of a knight. Edward was knighted by his father after the battle.

PRINCE EDWARD

EARL OF WARWICK

The ugly child

Bertrand du Guesclin was the son of a nobleman in Brittany, northern France. Despite having a beautiful mother, poor Bertrand was an ugly child who grew up to be a strong, thick-set man. He won a prize in a wrestling contest at Rennes, but his family was so disgusted that he had fought with just his bare fists that he swore never to fight again without knightly weapons. He entered his first tournament in disguise and broke fifteen lances before his father appeared unexpectedly against him. Bertrand refused to fight his father out of respect.

Bertrand fought bravely during the Hundred Years War and was knighted in 1354 after foiling an ambush set up by the English forces. He was thirty-four years old when he became a knight.

BERTRAND DU GUESCLIN

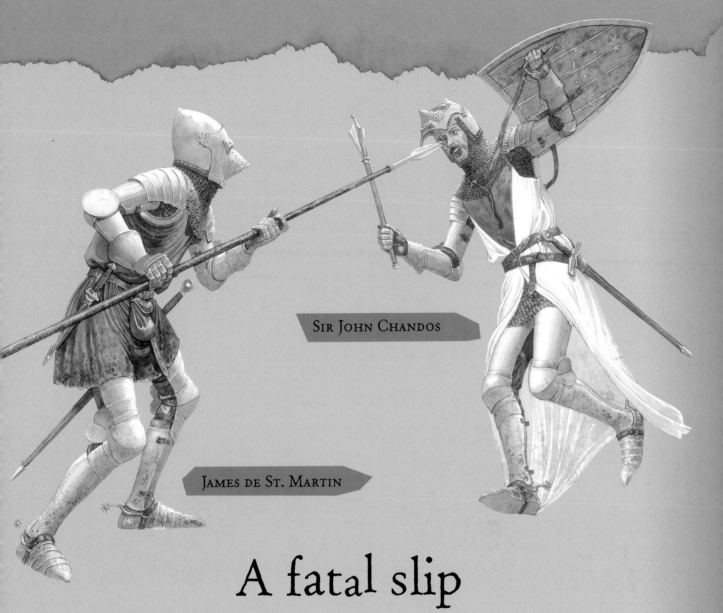

Sir John Chandos

James de St. Martin

A fatal slip

S ir John Chandos was one of the
most famous knights of the Middle
Ages: he was awarded the Order of
the Garter by Edward III because of his
great chivalry and bravery. He was a friend
of the king's son, the Black Prince, and
fought next to him at the battle of Poitiers
against King John of France. Sir John
Chandos carried on fighting until 1370,
when his career was cut short by a cruel
twist of fate. At Mortemer in France, he

and his men were fighting the enemy on
foot, but a morning frost had made the
ground slippery. His legs became
entangled in his long robe and he tripped.
A strong French squire called James de St.
Martin thrust at him with a lance. Sir John
did not see the lance coming because he
had lost an eye five years earlier while
hunting a stag. The lance hit Sir John
below that eye, he fell onto the sharp
point and died shortly after.

Medieval surgery

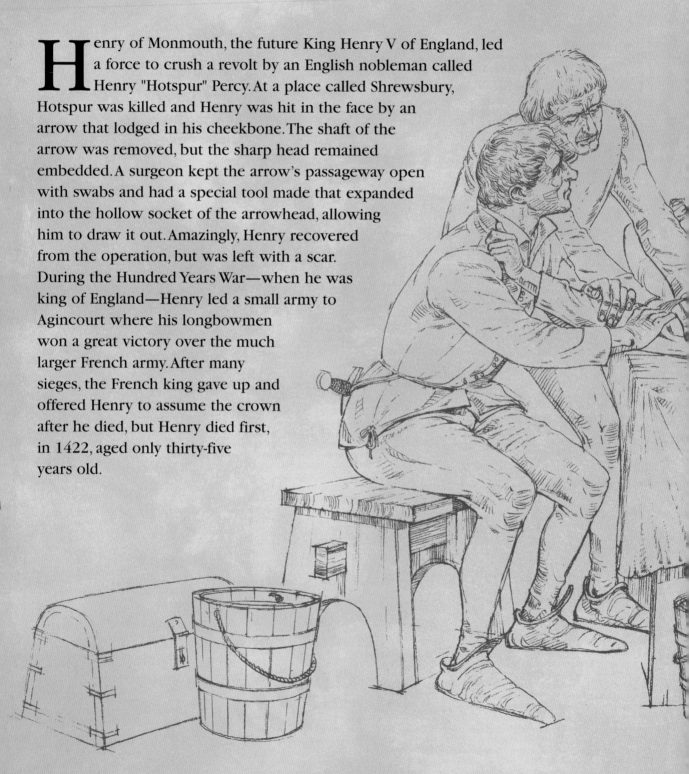

Henry of Monmouth, the future King Henry V of England, led a force to crush a revolt by an English nobleman called Henry "Hotspur" Percy. At a place called Shrewsbury, Hotspur was killed and Henry was hit in the face by an arrow that lodged in his cheekbone. The shaft of the arrow was removed, but the sharp head remained embedded. A surgeon kept the arrow's passageway open with swabs and had a special tool made that expanded into the hollow socket of the arrowhead, allowing him to draw it out. Amazingly, Henry recovered from the operation, but was left with a scar. During the Hundred Years War—when he was king of England—Henry led a small army to Agincourt where his longbowmen won a great victory over the much larger French army. After many sieges, the French king gave up and offered Henry to assume the crown after he died, but Henry died first, in 1422, aged only thirty-five years old.

HENRY OF MONMOUTH

Food, clothing, & entertainment

Knights were aristocrats so they had better food than many other people. They drank good wines and ate white bread instead of the coarse brown bread of the lower classes. They were fond of meat, including venison, boar, and wild fowl, but ate hardly any vegetables. The main meal was taken during the late morning. For centuries, honey was the main sweetener—sugar was very expensive because it had to be imported from overseas.

Getting dressed

Clothing consisted of a linen shirt and drawers worn under tunics made of linen, wool, or silk, often with warm cloaks over them. Gold thread or even jewels were used for decoration. Early knights wore workmanlike knee-length tunics. By about 1400, young men often wore very short jackets that revealed their legs, which were clad in woolen or linen hose. Older men wore longer gowns.

THIS MID-FOURTEENTH-CENTURY KNIGHT WEARS A BUTTONED PADDED TUNIC CALLED A "GIPOUN" WITH A JEWELED SWORD BELT ON HIS HIPS.

THIS KNIGHT OF ABOUT 1450 WEARS A HAT WITH A LONG TAIL CALLED A "LIRIPIPE."

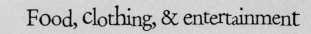

THE "GITTERN" WAS A KIND OF EARLY GUITAR.

EARLY KNIGHTS WORE SHORT TUNICS.

Time to relax

When they weren't fighting, knights liked to listen to songs, stories about love and adventure, and romances about heroes such as King Arthur. These might be sung to the accompaniment of the "gittern," an early guitar, or the lute. They watched tumblers, jugglers, and fire-eaters or played rough games. They also played wargames such as chess, chequers, and backgammon, and over the course of the Middle Ages more knights learned to read. Many loved to hunt or hawk, since this provided good exercise as well as extra food, and was the time they might use a bow or crossbow. They also trained with other knights or squires, or at the "quintain," a dummy target, and enjoyed watching and taking part in tournaments.

KNIGHTS LIKED TO EAT VENISON AND WILD BOAR.

THE LUTE CAME TO EUROPE FROM THE MIDDLE EAST IN THE THIRTEENTH CENTURY.

The Professionals

In the middle of the fourteenth century there was an outbreak of bubonic plague—known as the Black Death—that killed nearly half the population of western Europe. Partly as a result of this, the old feudal system declined. Lords found it more economical to hire soldiers for a set period, rather than having to support their knights even when they weren't fighting for him. In some parts of Europe, fighting men grouped themselves into companies that fought for money rather than out of loyalty to a lord. Many of these companies were found in Italy. The leaders of these mercenary soldiers were called *condottiere*. A few mercenaries remembered the chivalric code of conduct, but many were ruthless, with no thought for anything but their own ends. The old ideals were kept alive in books that told of chivalry and reminded men how a knight should behave.

"Needle John"

The English knight, Sir John Hawkwood, began his career as a tailor, which is how he got his nickname. When he grew bored with this work he became a soldier and took part in the Hundred Years War. He led a band of men who wore white clothing and were known as the "White Brotherhood," or the "White Company." When there was a break in the war in France, Hawkwood led his men to Italy where they would fight for whomever paid them the most money. Hawkwood spent a lot of time in Italy, joining different sides depending on who was most likely to win a campaign. He once cursed two friars who wished him peace: "Do you not know that I live by war and that peace would be my undoing?" As long as there were conflicts, Sir John and his men could earn a living!

"NEEDLE JOHN"

Pirate and knight!

In 1394, when Don Pero Niño was just fifteen years old, he took part in bullfights and jousted with cane lances. When he grew up, Pero Niño was the captain of a fleet of galleys that went in search of Muslim pirates (or "corsairs") along the Mediterranean coast of North Africa. He captured pirate ships and brought the treasure they held back to Spain. Pero Niño had crossbowmen on his ships. These men and their weapons were very effective in sea battles against the corsairs who were fierce fighters. Pero Niño was wounded in the leg by an arrow while attacking a Muslim vessel off the North African coast, but this didn't stop him. He attacked English lands in France and tried to capture ships as far away as the south-west coast of England!

Don Pero Niño

A paid fighter

Although Alberico da Barbiano was a *condottiere*—a mercenary leader rather than a man who fought for his lord—he believed that asking knights to dismount for battle was bad for their status. Alberico thought that a group of mounted men looked more impressive and so was more likely to be employed by a wealthy ruler! Alberico, who had learnt about warfare as a member of Sir John Hawkwood's "White Company," led the company of San Giorgio. Alberico became a respected leader in the 1370s and taught other *condottieri* how to train their men.

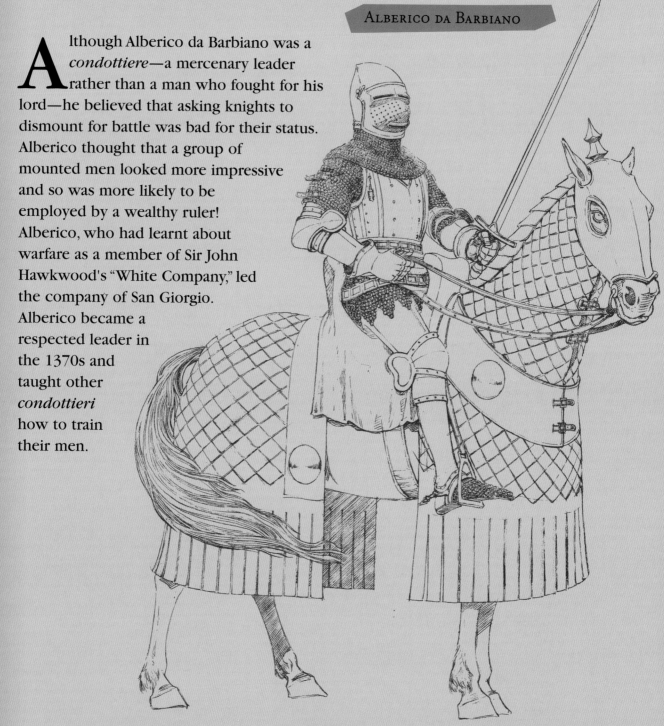

The man with an iron hand

Götz von Berlichingen

The German knight Götz von Berlichingen became known as "Götz of the Iron Hand" after he lost a hand at the siege of Landshut in 1504. A cannon shot ripped off his right hand and blasted his sword hilt in two, driving one half of the hilt and some pieces of his armor into his arm. He must have been a brave, tough man because he kept his wits and rode back to camp to find a surgeon! An armorer later made a false hand for him out of iron. Götz had fought for the Emperor Maximilian when he was only about sixteen years old. As a commander in charge of Landsknechts—tough professional soldiers who fought mainly on foot with long pikes— he took part in many wars in France and Switzerland. Although he was a knight, he also led a regiment of peasants in the German Peasants' War in 1524–26.

Tournaments

Tournaments began as training for war so real, sharp weapons were used. These team events or "tourneys" were violent clashes between two groups of mounted knights (and sometimes foot soldiers) that were held in open areas of countryside. In the thirteenth century, knights began using blunted weapons and the contests took place in a smaller, contained fighting area known as the "lists."

Jousting

As well as the tourney, single combat between two mounted knights with lances was becoming popular. These "jousts" gave the knight a better opportunity to show off his skill. Unhorsing your opponent earned points, as did striking his helmet or shield, or splintering your own lance against his body. "Jousts of peace" used blunted lances and special armor, including "frog-mouthed" helms designed to guide an opponent's lance away from the eyes. More daring knights preferred "jousts of war," which used sharp lances.

Tilting

The "tilt," or barrier, was introduced in the first half of the fifteenth century to prevent jousters from colliding. As ideas of courtly love developed, the influence of ladies also grew and some knights carried their lady's "favor" or token into combat to show their devotion.

ARMOR FOR A JOUST OF PEACE HAD A FROG-MOUTHED HELM TO PROTECT THE KNIGHT'S FACE.

Pageantry

Lords held tournaments to show off their power and gain popularity. Themes and popular legends were acted out, and pageantry became part of the event. Later, an increase in foot tournaments between teams of men with long spears or swords reflected changes in real warfare.

In this foot combat from about 1470, both knights use pollaxes.

These knights from about 1450 use blunt swords and clubs. The helmets have a grill at the front and large wood and leather crests on top.

Glossary

arming doublet *(p.12)* A lightly padded jacket worn under plate armor. Some doublets had full mail sleeves.

chivalry *(p.4, 22, 27, 35, 40)* A word meaning "horsemanship," since all early knights needed horses. From the twelfth century it became associated with courtly manners and love of ladies.

condotierre *(p.40, 44)* A mercenary who fought in Italy in the fourteeth and fifteenth centuries. Many *condottieri* formed themselves into companies of soldiers.

feudal system *(p.4, 6, 40)* A system that evolved in Europe in the eighth and ninth centuries, in which a man served his lord in return for protection and a piece of land to farm.

helm *(p.46, 47)* A helmet developed in the early thirteenth century that covered the whole head. At first flat-topped, it later became more conical or pointed. It had a vision slit or slits and breathing holes. Some later helms had a visor.

joust *(p.46)* Single combat between two mounted opponents. Jousts of peace used blunted lances; jousts of war had sharp lances.

knight A man of good birth and a member of a select group in society, who had undergone training and been knighted. In later centuries, members of the lower gentry began to receive knighthood, and even occasionally members of the lower classes.

lance *(p.13, 20, 21, 23, 34, 35, 42, 46)* A long, sharp spear carried by a horseman. By about 1100, most knights tucked their lances under one arm as they charged their enemy on horseback.

lists *(p.46)* The enclosure in which the actual combat in a tournament took place. Also the word for the fences around the enclosure.

Order of the Garter *(p.35)* King Edward III introduced this order of knighthood around 1348, making it the oldest in Europe.

page *(p.6)* A boy, sometimes as young as seven, who was in training to become a squire, then a knight.

pike *(p.21, 45)* A very long spear with a small head.

pollaxe *(p.13, 47)* A weapon consisting of a wooden pole with an axe blade backed by a hammer and topped by a spike; some pollaxes had a hammer backed by a sharp beak instead.

squire *(p.6, 10, 12, 20, 35, 39)* The rank below that of knight. In the early Middle Ages, squires were often servants but it also referred to the sons of knights in training. From the thirteenth century, squires sometimes refused to become knights because of the cost and the extra work in government. Thus many older men remained squires.

surcoat *(p.12)* A cloth covering over armor that appeared around 1150. Once full, plate armor appeared around 1400 many knights stopped wearing them.

tournament *(p.6, 11, 24, 27, 34, 39, 46-47)* A spectacle that developed from practice for war, probably in the twelfth century. From the fourteenth century, three forms were in use: the tourney or team event; jousts or single mounted combats; and foot combats usually between two men.

Index